KATE GREENAWAY

Kate Greenaway — Engraving by H. Thiriat

KATE GREENAWAY

ACADEMY EDITIONS·LONDON

ACKNOWLEDGEMENTS

Thanks are due to the private collectors and to the Victoria and Albert Museum for permission to photograph and reproduce works in their collections.

A full bibliography is given in *Kate Greenaway* by Rodney K. Engen, Academy Editions, London.

First published in Great Britain by
Academy Editions, 7 Holland Street London W8

© 1977 Academy Editions

ISBN 85670 358 3

Printed and bound in Great Britain by
Acolortone Ltd., Ipswich

Kate Greenaway was born in London on 17th March 1846, daughter of wood-engraver John Greenaway. The world into which she was born had already been scarred by industrialisation; the energies of wind, wood and water had been replaced by coal. It was an age of railway-mania, an age of Dickensian urban poverty, an age of steam of smoke, and for many an age of sorrow. It seemed to the Victorians that those traditional values of modesty, religiousness, craftsmanship, and a certain delicacy of feeling, were being undermined as quickly as the landscape was changing.

Kate Greenaway was fortunate. Although her family was not wealthy, she had a comfortable and stable childhood, and while she lived mainly in London, two early years and several holidays were spent on a Nottinghamshire farm, where her appreciation of natural beauty was no doubt formed. The sentiments of her Little London Girl in *Marigold Garden* —

> 'Oh, I'll stay in the country, and make a daisy chain
> And never go back to London again' —

must echo what she herself felt as a child towards the temporary pleasures of country life. It is possibly a reflection on her serious and diligent attitude towards her own work as an illustrator that, after leaving the Slade School of Art, Kate Greenaway chose to remain in London in order to pursue her career by undertaking commissions for *The Illustrated London News,* greetings cards, and children's novels.

It was on the basis of these early drawings that Kate Greenaway's reputation as an illustrator grew. The Christmas card, first conceived in the year of her birth, had become a craze by the 1870s, and the sensitive way in which Kate Greenaway approached the Christmas theme intensified demand for the cards, and for her work. She introduced her particular world of angelic children to a public hungry for old fashioned prettiness and sentimental escapism.

It was not, however, until the publication of *Under the Window* in 1878, that Kate Greenaway's talents were fully realized. This book, printed in colour by the expert Edmund Evans using a special wood block process he had developed himself, was the first in which Kate Greenaway could allow her imagination free rein, as she had not only drawn the illustrations but also written the rhymes. She no longer had to use her time and ability to illuminate borders or produce over-elaborate designs which were contracted into the corners of cards. She could now concentrate on full page, colour pictures, in which the decoration formed an integral part of the picture design.

The style and sensibility of Kate Greenaway's subsequent work were established in *Under the Window.* It was her particular depiction of children and the world in which she placed them that captured the popular imagination throughout England, France (where the term *Greenawisme* was coined), and America. Her vision of a 'clear-eyed, soft-faced happy-hearted childhood . . . the coy reticences, the simplicities, and the small solemnities of the little people,' was admired by Austin Dobson in an 1880 review of the Fine Arts Society exhibition of the *Under the Window* drawings. Children were, to the Victorians, miniature adults. Kate Greenaway portrays them in all the attitudes of adult life — having tea, walking out, in solitary contemplation — and always with solemn, absorbed faces, yet retaining the innocence and simplicity of childhood. In all her work only the Little Fat Goblin (a 'notable sinner') in *Under the Window,* the naughty April Fool boy in *The Birthday Book,* her witches and a few adults — being perhaps undeserving — are not endowed with the soft curls, the round, rosy cheeks, the determinedly pointed chins and the sexless prettiness which became her hallmark. She endeared herself to parents by presenting an image of exemplary behaviour. Her children are seldom naughty, never dirty. Like the genteel family in *Marigold Garden,*

> 'They put on gloves when they go out,
> And run not in the street,
> And on wet days not one of them
> Had ever muddy feet.'

Probably the most notable indication of Kate Greenaway's popularity during her own lifetime is the rapidity with which not only her books and her style of illustration, but also the clothes in which her children were dressed, became fashionable. With a nostalgia typical of the times, and with an attention to detail characteristic of her work, Kate Greenaway made imitation eighteenth century frocks, smocks, aprons, ribbons, bonnets and wide brimmed hats in which to clothe her young models, thereby setting the fashion for children's dress wherever her books were popular.

Kate Greenaway placed her young and fashionable cherubs in a landscape which was uniquely English, if somewhat idealised. Her children are nearly always out of doors, nearly always in a countryside tamed with fences, flower-beds and mellow brick walls. It was the garden rather than the wild and open land that inspired Kate Greenaway. When she chose an urban setting it was never dark or dreary, but rather an attempt at the mediaevalism which was part of the Victorian ideal, with spires and turrets rising up above the rooftops. *The Pied Piper of Hamelin* offered her the full expression of the mediaeval vision. Her interiors are fresh and homely. Whatever her background, there are always flowers, whether growing in the grass, spilling out of baskets, woven into tablecloths, or forming decorative arches or corners. There is nowhere a trace of industrial life; in the words of her great friend and admirer John Ruskin, there were no railroads 'to carry the children away with . . . no tunnel or pit mouth to swallow them up . . . no vestige, in fact, of science, civilisation, economical arrangements, or commercial enterprise!' Her world is totally innocent, and in this lies its appeal.

Kate Greenaway identified strongly with children, though she remained a spinster throughout her life. She felt that her particular blend of reality and idealism 'a very real thing mixed up with a great unreality,' was something that would excite children's imagination. It is this blend, the 'giving something to nature that is possible for nature to have, but always has not,' as she put it, that places Kate Greenaway firmly within the aesthetic tradition of her age. To the Victorians, the purest reality was nature tamed and beautified, but not exploited.

Stylistically, Kate Greenaway's work combines the intricate detail of the Pre-Raphaelites, which she greatly admired, with the careful design and simple composition of the Aesthetic Movement. Her sense of balance, already evident in *Under the Window,* had become firmly disciplined and extremely sensitive with the publication of the *Book of Games* in 1889. Her colouring, gradually refined through constant effort and study of colour harmony, soon became subtle and delicate, with an emphasis on pastel shades which retain an intensity through the use of black outlines and little shading. Her draughtsmanship, criticised at times by the honest Ruskin who persuaded her to practise life studies, improved greatly after *The Birthday Book* in 1880. Her figures began to move more naturally, her sharp ground shadows became subdued, her lines became even finer and more delicate, and taking note of Ruskin's advice that, 'the *first thing* you have to do in this leafy world is to learn to paint a leaf green, or its full size,' she took infinite care in the realistic representation of every detail in her pictures. It was said at the time that nobody could draw flowers more beautifully or more convincingly than 'K.G.,' as she was called. Much of the power of Kate Greenaway's design, in particular the arrangements of branches and blossom, the restrained use of shading, and its simplicity, can be attributed to the influence of Japan, recently opened to the outside world and a fresh source of inspiration to many Victorians.

The April Baby's Book of Tunes was published in 1900, a successful venture despite the fact that Kate Greenaway was losing her health and, albeit temporarily, her popularity. In 1881 a reviewer in *The Times* had found a 'lackadaisical prettiness of style' in her latest work. The opinion was not, at the time, shared. But with the turning of the century and the passing of the Victorian era it became clear to Kate Greenaway that a new and more sophisticated generation of illustrators, epitomised by Aubrey Beardsley, was taking her place in the public imagination. Remaining confident in her belief that 'a face should look like a face and a beautiful arm like a beautiful arm,' she was distressed by the new vision of the young 'modern' artists. 'People laugh,' she had written to author Austin Dobson, '. . . have I a defective art faculty that few things are ugly to me?' Whether her rose-tinted view of the world was due to a lack of critical ability, an inherent innocence and simplicity, or the blindness that was vital to the Victorian sensibility, it is a tribute to Kate Greenaway's talents as an illustrator that even now, in an age dominated on the one hand by abstraction and on the other by an almost dogmatic realism, Kate Greenaway remains a favourite amongst children and adults.

THE PIED PIPER OF HAMELIN
A poem by Robert Browning
London, 1888

1

'. . . To see the townsfolk suffer so
From vermin, was a pity.'

THE PIED PIPER OF HAMELIN

2

'At last the people in a body
To the Town Hall came flocking . . . '

At last the people in a body
    To the Town Hall came flocking:
"'Tis clear," cried they, "our Mayor's a noddy;
    "And as for our Corporation—shocking

THE PIED PIPER OF HAMELIN

3

'Out came the children running.'

4

overleaf
'All the little boys and girls,
... ran merrily after,
The wonderful music with shouting and laughter.'

Tripping and skipping, ran merrily after

The wonderful music with shouting and laughter.

THE PIED PIPER OF HAMELIN

5

'And Piper and dancers were gone for ever, . . . '

UNDER THE WINDOW
Pictures and rhymes by Kate Greenaway
London, 1885

6

May Blossom

7

Phillis and Belinda

8

'Poor Dicky's dead!'

9

'School is over,
Oh, what fun!'

10

The fat little Goblin

This little fat Goblin,
  A notable sinner,
Stole cabbages daily,
  For breakfast and dinner.

The Farmer looked sorry;
  He cried, and with pain,
"That rogue has been here
  For his cabbage again!"

That little plump Goblin,
  He laughed, "Ho! ho! ha!
Before me he catches,
  He'll have to run far."

That little fat Goblin,
  He never need sorrow;
He stole three to-day,
  And he'll steal more to-morrow.

11
Tommy

Tommy was a silly boy.
  "I can fly," he said ;
He started off, but very soon
  He tumbled on his head.

His little sister Prue was there,
  To see how he would do it ;
She knew that, after all his boast,
  Full dearly Tom would rue it !

K.G

MARIGOLD GARDEN
Pictures and rhymes by Kate Greenaway
London, 1885

12

Book cover

MARIGOLD GARDEN

13
Frontispiece

14

The Tea Party

MARIGOLD GARDEN

15
Susan Blue

SUSAN BLUE.

OH, Susan Blue,
How do you do?
Please may I go for a walk with you?
Where shall we go?
Oh, I know—
Down in the meadow where the cowslips grow!

MARIGOLD GARDEN

16

Street Show

STREET SHOW.

PUFF, puff, puff. How the trumpets blow.

All you little boys and girls come and see
    the show.

One — two — three, the Cat runs up the
    tree ;

But the little Bird he flies away—

"She hasn't got me !"

17

My Little Girlie

MY LITTLE GIRLIE.

LITTLE girlie tell to me
What your wistful blue eyes see?
Why you like to stand so high,
Looking at the far-off sky.

Does a tiny Fairy flit
In the pretty blue of it?
Or is it that you hope so soon
To see the rising yellow Moon?

Or is it—as I think I've heard—
You're looking for a little Bird
To come and sit upon a spray,
And sing the summer night away?

18

Going to see Grandmamma

GOING TO SEE GRANDMAMMA.

LITTLE Molly and Damon
  Are walking so far,
For they're going to see
  Their kind Grandmamma.

And they very well know,
  When they get there she'll take
From out of her cupboard
  Some very nice cake.

And into her garden
  They know they may run,
And pick some red currants,
  And have lots of fun.

So Damon to doggie
  Says, " How do you do ? "
And asks his mamma
  If he may not go too.

19

The Four Princesses

THE FOUR PRINCESSES.

FOUR Princesses lived in a Green Tower—
   A Bright Green Tower in the middle of the sea;
And no one could think—oh, no one could think—
   Who the Four Princesses could be.

One looked to the North, and one to the South,
   And one to the East, and one to the West;
They were all so pretty, so very pretty,
   You could not tell which was the prettiest.

20

The Ungrateful Lamb

THE UNGRATEFUL LAMB.

KATE GREENAWAY'S BOOK OF GAMES
London, 1889

21

Battledore and Shuttlecock

BATTLEDORE & SHUTTLECOCK.

THIS is a most convenient game, because one solitary individual can find amusement as well as any number, provided there is a bat for each player. The object of the game is to keep the shuttlecock going as long as possible.

22

Skipping

SKIPPING.

Two children each hold one end
of a rope, and stand so that in turning it just
touches the ground in the middle. How fast
they turn entirely depends on the skipper. Two
can skip at the same time over the rope if it
is a fairly long one. In skipping singly it is
more graceful to watch if the rope is thrown
backwards over the head rather
than forward under the feet.

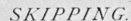

23

Tom Tiddler's Ground

24

Kites

25

Cover for Almanack for 1884

26

Cover for Almanack for 1890

ALMANACK

FOR

1890

BY KATE GREENAWAY

27

Back cover for Almanack for 1890

28

Calendar for 1884

KATE GREENAWAY'S CALENDAR FOR 1884

29

A Calendar of the Seasons for 1876
Spring

CALENDAR OF THE SEASONS for 1876

MARCUS WARD & CO LONDON & BELFAST

30

A Calendar of the Seasons for 1876
Summer

MARCUS WARD & CO. LONDON & BELFAST

31

A Calendar of the Seasons for 1876
Autumn

MARCUS WARD & CO LONDON & BELFAST

32

A Calendar of the Seasons for 1876
Winter

CALENDAR OF THE SEASONS FOR 1876

MARCUS WARD & CO. LONDON & BELFAST

33

Christmas Card

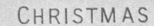

CHRISTMAS

Warmest greetings,
Happy meetings,
Be thy lot to-day;
Joys unending,
With love blending,
Never pass away!

(COPYRIGHT)

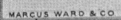

34
New Year Card

NEW
YEAR

Emblem of grace and joy,
I send this blossom fair;
So may thy life alway
Be sweet with fragrance rare!

(COPYRIGHT)

MARCUS WARD & CO

35

New Year Card

LET ME WHISPER IN YOUR EAR
A PROMISE FROM THE KIND NEW YEAR

36

Greetings Card

I'VE GOT SUCH A STORE OF PRESENTS FOR YOU
I FANCY THAT WE SHALL BE FRIENDS, WE TWO

MARCUS WARD & CO.

37
Valentine Card

KISS ME FOR I LOVE YOU SO
WITHOUT A KISS YOU SHALL NOT GO.

38
Greetings Card

MIRTH AND JOY FOR TO-DAY SHOULD BE
THEREFORE I BRING THIS CUP TO THEE.

39
Valentine Card

40
Valentine Card

41
Valentine Card

42
Valentine Card

43
Greetings Card

K.G.

44

Greetings Card

45

Greetings Card

APRIL BABY'S BOOK OF TUNES
London, 1900

46

Sing a Song of Sixpence

KATE GREENAWAY'S BIRTHDAY BOOK FOR CHILDREN
London, 1880

47
April

BIRTHDAY BOOK

48
October

BIRTHDAY BOOK

49
December

BIRTHDAY BOOK

50

August